The Second World War

Usborne Quicklinks

The Usborne Quicklinks Website is packed with thousands of links to all the best websites on the internet. The websites include information, video clips, sounds, games and animations that support and enhance the information in Usborne internet-linked books.

To visit the recommended websites for this book, go to the Usborne Quicklinks Website at **www.usborne-quicklinks.com** and enter the keywords **History of Britain**, then click on **The Second World War**.

When using the internet please follow the internet safety guidelines displayed on the Usborne Quicklinks Website. The recommended websites in Usborne Quicklinks are regularly reviewed and updated, but Usborne Publishing Ltd. is not responsible for the content or availability of any website other than its own. We recommend that children are supervised while using the internet.

The Second World War

Henry Brook

Illustrated by Ian McNee

Designed by Tom Lalonde, Stephen Moncrieff
& Steve Wood

Edited by
Ruth Brocklehurst
& Jane Chisholm

Consultant: Terry Charman,
Imperial War Museum

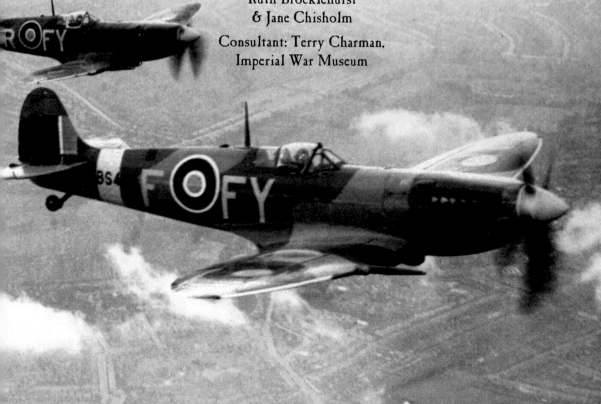

Contents

Britain at war

Barely twenty years after the horrors of the
First World War, German tanks stormed
across Europe and started the bloodiest and most
pitiless conflict ever seen. The Second World War
was a global battle for survival – for most of the
nations involved, their citizens and their way of life.
  Britain's Prime Minister, Winston Churchill,
called on every man, woman and child to join the
fight. After six years of terrible fighting alongside
their allies, the British won
victory and the chance
to help shape the
modern world.

Hitler's Germany

Adolf Hitler and his extreme racist Nazi Party came to power in 1933.

The Nazis believed that people of pure Germanic blood were a 'master race' – superior to other races. They built up the German army so that they could conquer a new empire in Europe.

Hitler blamed the Jews living in Germany for the country's economic problems. As a result, they faced increasing persecution and violence, and many were driven from their jobs and their homes.

No choice but war

The 1930s had been desperate years in Britain and across Europe. Economic depression forced millions into poverty, while ruthless politicians preached hate and violence to angry crowds looking for someone to blame. But war might have been avoided, if it hadn't been for the rage of a single, terrifying man – Adolf Hitler.

Hitler felt betrayed by the German surrender after the First World War. Using cunning and brute force, he seized political control in Germany and built up a powerful army. World leaders looked on in despair as Hitler sent troops to the French border and into Austria. When he threatened to invade a region of Czechoslovakia, it became clear to Germany's old enemies, Britain and France, that they would have to take action to maintain peace in Europe.

Appeasement and betrayal

To most people in Britain, the political problems in Europe seemed a long way away. They had problems of their own, and were in no mood to fight. Desperate to avoid war, the British Prime Minister, Neville Chamberlain, met Hitler at Munich in September 1938. They were joined by Edouard Daladier and Benito Mussolini, the French and Italian heads of government.

The four agreed that Hitler could take Sudetenland – part of Czechoslovakia with a large German population. In return, Hitler promised not to invade any more territories.

Hitler gave rousing speeches about the 'master race' at massive rallies.

A broken promise

But Chamberlain had been tricked. Hitler's tanks swarmed into the rest of Czechoslovakia too, and on September 1, 1939, they crashed across Poland. Applying speed and overwhelming firepower, in a new style of attack known as *Blitzkrieg* or lightning war, Hitler's generals smashed the Polish army in less than a month. The time for making peace was over.

On September 3, Chamberlain made a radio speech telling the British people that they were at war with Germany. Only minutes later, air raid sirens sounded across London.

"My good friends, for the second time in our history, a British Prime Minister has returned from Germany bringing peace with honour. I believe it is peace for our time."

Neville Chamberlain announces the Munich Peace Agreement to the people of Britain.

A jubilant Chamberlain returns from Munich, waving a signed peace agreement between Britain and Germany. Just six months later, Hitler would disregard it.

Action stations

"Always have your
gas mask with you
– day and night.
Learn to put it
on quickly."

This advice, from the
Ministry of Home
Security to the people of
Britain, was published in
the Sunday newspapers.

The first air raid warning over London was a false
alarm. But, even so, there was an atmosphere of fear
across the city. Britain's Royal Navy was strong, but the
country was badly prepared for war.

Thousands of men and women throughout Britain
decided that now was the time to 'do their bit' to
defend their country. Many joined the ARP – Air Raid
Precautions – as wardens. Most ARP wardens were
unpaid volunteers, and their chief task was to make
sure everybody knew what to do during an air raid.
They sounded sirens to warn of an imminent raid and
looked after public shelters.

At dusk, every city light was put out or covered up,
to stop bomber crews from spotting targets. This
was called the blackout, and the wardens made
sure it was strictly enforced.

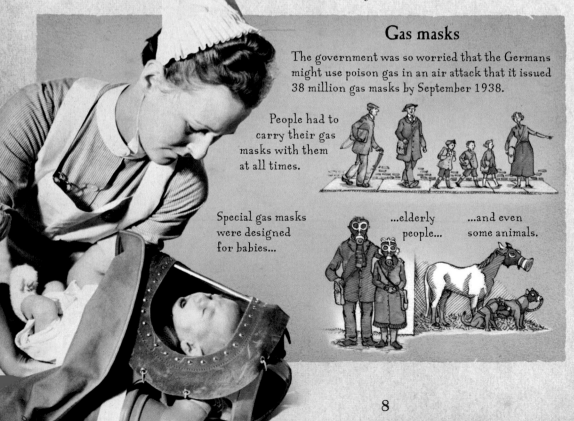

Gas masks

The government was so worried that the Germans
might use poison gas in an air attack that it issued
38 million gas masks by September 1938.

People had to
carry their gas
masks with them
at all times.

Special gas masks
were designed
for babies...

...elderly
people...

...and even
some animals.

Preparing for war

The country was finally gearing up for war. Young men were conscripted (called up for compulsory service) into the armed forces and Chamberlain ordered his generals to send a force to France. He also appointed Winston Churchill, a tough veteran of the First World War, to take charge of the Royal Navy.

Two days before Chamberlain's radio speech, a massive evacuation project was set in motion, as millions of children from Britain's cities were moved to the countryside, to try to escape the bombers. Most went by train, moving across a landscape that was rapidly changing in the face of war.

All over the country, the nation waited anxiously, wondering when the first air raids would strike – but nothing happened.

There were lots of accidents during the blackout. This poster warns people to let their eyes adjust before going out in the dark.

This ARP warden (with W for warden marked on his helmet) is directing a family to the nearest air raid shelter during a drill.

The Germans first used *Blitzkrieg* against Poland. This is how the tactic worked:

First, bombers attacked enemy air bases, military headquarters, ammunition depots and train stations.

Next, Stuka dive bombers swooped in machine-gunning and bombing enemy front line troops...

...and paratroopers made surprise raids.

Then, tanks broke through, calling in dive bombers to help clear any obstacles.

Enemy groups were then surrounded and crushed, while the main attack force advanced.

The fall of western Europe

After Hitler's whirlwind success in Poland, the fighting came to a standstill, during the winter months. Hitler's army was sitting tight inside Poland, no bombs had fallen on Britain, and by January 1940, most of the children who had been evacuated from the cities had returned home.

The phoney war

As the months went by, people began talking about a "phoney" war and some British politicians thought it might still be possible to arrange a peace. But, although no shots were fired on land, there was savage fighting at sea. A German U-boat submarine sank the battleship, *Royal Oak*, and almost a thousand British sailors drowned. Two months later, off the coast South America, the German warship, *Admiral Graf Spee*, was hunted down by the British and scuttled by its own crew, to prevent it from being captured.

Lightning strikes

On April 9, Hitler put an end to all talk of peace by launching *Blitzkrieg* against Denmark and Norway. Next, his tanks broke through at a weak point in France's northern frontier. The Germans kept advancing, using paratrooper landings and Stuka raids to spread panic before them. In six weeks they had overwhelmed the French, and pushed the British army onto the beaches around Dunkirk. The seven-month phoney war was over, and the British had suffered what would turn out to be one of the greatest military disasters of the war.

German Stukas sweep across the sky in formation. These black, gull-shaped dive bombers had sirens fitted under the wings. They made a terrifying screech as they dived, causing panic, even among experienced soldiers.

This map shows Europe in summer 1940, by which time much of Western Europe and Scandinavia was under Nazi occupation.

NORWAY

DENMARK

UK
NETHERLANDS
Dunkirk BELGIUM
GERMANY
FRANCE
CZECHOSLOVAKIA
AUSTRIA
ITALY
POLAND

SOVIET
UNION
(formerly
Russia)

Friends and enemies

Allies:
Britain and its empire, France and Poland, were joined, in December 1941, by the United States.

Axis Powers:
Germany, Italy and Japan

Areas under Axis control by summer 1940

Neutral countries
The Soviet Union announced its neutrality before the war and agreed not to attack Germany in return for a share of land in Poland. Later, Hitler attacked the Soviets, who then joined the Allies.

Maginot Line
The French built this line of fortified trenches along the German border to prevent an invasion. The plan failed when Hitler's tanks simply stormed around it.

In a typically defiant
pose, Winston Churchill
inspects a Thompson
submachine gun, or
'Tommy' gun, during a
tour of England's
northeastern coast,
August, 1940.

Warrior Winston

As *Blitzkrieg* blazed across France, many people wondered if the war was lost already. Chamberlain was blamed for the crisis and was forced to resign, opening the way for the old soldier and statesman, Winston Churchill, to become Prime Minister on May 10, 1940.

No surrender

Churchill was already in his mid-sixties when he became Prime Minister, and he had had his share of adventures. He came from an aristocratic family, inheriting an upper-class lifestyle, but without the money to go with it. Before going into politics, he'd served in the army, supporting himself mainly by writing war reports. He was involved in the Anglo-Boer War, and the First World War, and witnessed battles across four continents. Gruff and tough, Churchill brushed aside any talk of making peace with Germany. In an astonishing speech to the House of Commons, he promised to lead the country in a fight to the death, rather than surrender.

"You ask, what is our aim? I can answer in one word: it is victory... for without victory, there is no survival... no survival for the British Empire, no survival for all that the British Empire has stood for..."

Winston Churchill, May 13, 1940

ALL BEHIND YOU, WINSTON

This picture was drawn by the cartoonist David Low, the week Churchill became Prime Minister. It shows him as a man of action who has inspired the support of the entire nation.

Tough talk

For years, Churchill had been warning of the dangers posed by Hitler and his Nazi political party – and now that German tanks were pushing the army back towards the English Channel, the dangers seemed all too real. In a speech on becoming Prime Minister, he laid out what people could expect in the coming months: "I have nothing to offer but blood, toil, tears and sweat. We have before us an ordeal of the most grievous kind."

But despite this gloomy prediction, Churchill was confident of final victory. He believed the Royal Navy could defend his island nation from attack and was convinced that America and the Soviet Union would eventually join the fight against Hitler.

In a series of electrifying speeches, Churchill won over the British public with his boldness and defiance, bracing them for the greatest struggle of their lives.

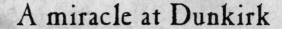

A miracle at Dunkirk

On May 24, 1940, the British army and thousands of their French and Belgian allies were trapped at Dunkirk, facing capture or annihilation. Hitler sent the German airforce, the *Luftwaffe*, to destroy the crowded port. In response, Churchill ordered an emergency evacuation, codenamed Operation Dynamo. He expected the Royal Navy to bring back only one tenth of his army. But, against all odds, the Dunkirk rescue turned into a breathtaking triumph.

Hot water

British, French and Belgian troops were still streaming into Dunkirk when the rescue began. They were greeted by a shocking vision of tens of thousands of men scattered across the beaches, waiting to be rescued.

Thick smoke from the burning city gave them some protection from German planes, but the sea was still full of wrecked ships and drowned soldiers. The water by the beach was too shallow for big ships to sail close to the shore, so the men had to wait in line to reach a long pier. Others waded out to waiting rescue ships, or rowed out on small boats. Shells and bullets exploded around them, and they risked being attacked by Stukas as they moved slowly out to sea.

Up to their necks in water, these British soldiers are wading out from the beach at Dunkirk to reach a waiting rescue ship.

The little ships

To speed things up, the Royal Navy needed a huge number of smaller ships to collect soldiers directly from the beach. Over 700 river boats, pleasure cruisers and fishing boats made the journey across the English Channel. Most were crewed by navy sailors, but some civilian boat owners came along as volunteers. They risked their lives, picking men out of the waves and ferrying them to larger ships.

These are just a few of the 'little ships' that took part in the Dunkirk evacuation.

Fight another day

In nine days, the Royal Navy's rescue fleet carried almost 340,000 soldiers to safety. German generals were furious that an enemy army had slipped through their fingers, while in Britain people celebrated the return of their husbands, sons and friends. Every fighting man would be needed, if Hitler gave the order to invade.

"Wars are not won by evacuations."

Winston Churchill warns people that the war is not over yet.

Enemy occupation

Churchill's army had escaped, but the Germans still managed to snatch a piece of Britain. Just weeks after the evacuation of Dunkirk, German troops occupied the Channel Islands.

Churchill had already evacuated thousands of islanders, having decided that the islands couldn't be defended without heavy loss of life. Those who stayed behind now had to adjust to life under the Nazis.

Islanders were issued with identity cards and German money.

Their radios were seized, but some hid them and continued to listen to the BBC in secret.

The Germans fortified Jersey and Guernsey with gun emplacements and lookout posts that still stare out to sea today.

The Battle of Britain

Just three weeks after Dunkirk, France surrendered and Hitler's conquering army began drawing up plans to invade England. Protected by its moat of stormy sea and the mighty Royal Navy, the British Isles had fought off invaders for almost 900 years. But, if the Germans won control of the skies, they could bomb the British out of the water, clearing the way for their landing craft. Through a blazing hot summer, Britain's fighter pilots struggled desperately to save their country.

On July 10, 1940, the 'Battle of Britain' started, with *Luftwaffe* bombers attacking ships and airbases along the southern coast of England. Their plan was simple: to lure Britain's RAF – Royal Air Force – fighter planes into the sky and shoot them down. They thought the RAF could be destroyed within a week.

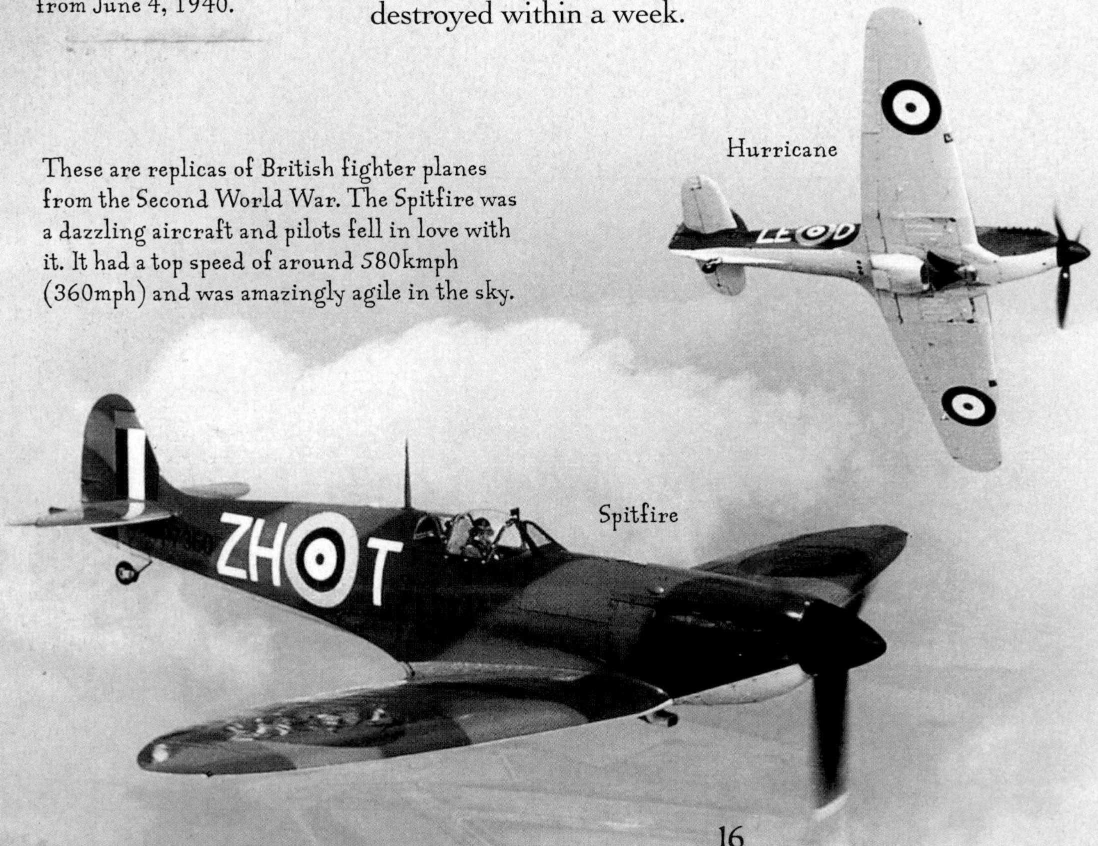

Hurricane

These are replicas of British fighter planes from the Second World War. The Spitfire was a dazzling aircraft and pilots fell in love with it. It had a top speed of around 580kmph (360mph) and was amazingly agile in the sky.

Spitfire

16

This Messerschmitt Me 109 was the *Luftwaffe*'s principal fighter plane during the Battle of Britain.

Tracking the enemy

The *Luftwaffe* had over 2,000 planes and skilled pilots to fly them, but they had underestimated the RAF. In the build-up to war, RAF scientists had built a network of radar stations to guard their coast. Using powerful radio signals, radar equipment spotted and tracked any planes crossing the English Channel. This helped RAF commanders to position their fighters carefully and block enemy raids.

Home ground

British Hurricane and Spitfire fighter planes could hold their own against German aircraft and, because they were flying over home turf, RAF pilots could quickly land to refuel and re-arm their machines. If they were attacked and had to parachute to safety, they came down among friends and might be flying another plane within hours.

But the RAF's greatest strength had nothing to do with radar or flying machines – it was the fighting spirit of its airmen.

Off duty

Airmen from other Allied countries fought with the RAF. It was a multinational air force and some of its best flyers came from Poland and Czechoslovakia.

RAF pilots led something of a double-life during the battle. In the daytime they were out blasting at enemy planes and trying to stay alive. But at night, they came back to base and could pop into a local bar for a glass of beer and a game of darts.

RAF pilot Ray Holmes became an overnight hero when he was involved in a dramatic fight above London.

Holmes spotted a German Dornier bomber heading for Buckingham Palace. He tried to shoot the plane down, but found he had run out of ammunition.

Determined to save the palace, he rammed the bomber, slicing through its tail and ripping its wings off.

The German plane crashed just outside Victoria train station.

Holmes jumped from his broken plane and made a parachute landing in someone's back yard.

Miraculously, no civilians were hurt, and Holmes was soon back in action.

A few good men

When the Battle of Britain began, the RAF had just over 600 fighter planes to defend the country against the *Luftwaffe*'s 2,000. The British pilots – who became known as 'The Few' – were often young, fresh out of school, and many had never flown into battle before. But they had good reasons to fight hard. While *Luftwaffe* pilots were just doing their job, RAF flyers were struggling to save their homes and families from destruction.

Spitfire summer

The Battle of Britain raged through a searing July and August, as *Luftwaffe* bombers pounded Britain's airports, radar stations and landing strips. Between sorties, RAF pilots lounged in the grass, trying to keep cool and rest until a siren or bell sent them sprinting to their planes again. They were only given minutes to take off and climb high into the clouds before intercepting the enemy raiders.

No mercy

People on the ground stopped to watch the clash in the skies, but they had no idea of the speed and ferocity of the fighting. Enemy planes passed in a dizzying blur, as pilots tried to fire short bursts at each other from machine guns set into the wings of their fighters. It was a savage and bloody contest, with little mercy shown on either side. Almost one in five of the 3,000 RAF airmen who took part in the Battle of Britain was killed in the struggle.

A first victory

But, by late September, the *Luftwaffe* accepted that their mission to crush the RAF had failed. Despite taking a terrible battering, the British pilots had always managed to keep fighting. It was Britain's first victory in the war, and it sent a message of hope around the country.

"Never, in the field of human conflict, was so much owed by so many to so few."

Churchill describes the sacrifice and bravery of the RAF's airmen.

This photograph of RAF pilots appeared on a poster produced to celebrate the achievements of the Air Force in the Battle of Britain.

In areas that were under threat from air raids, people were given 'Anderson shelters' to build in their back yards.

Anderson shelters were designed to sleep six people. They were made from curved sheets of corrugated iron, half buried, with earth piled on top.

But many more people ended up taking refuge in public shelters, including ones in underground stations.

Hell came to London

On September 7, 1940, a black cloud of almost 1,000 German warplanes attacked London. By nightfall, the docklands and some of the eastern districts were ablaze and the sky glowed red. At dawn, Londoners saw a great cloud of thick smoke looming over their city. Having failed to crush the RAF, the German *Luftwaffe* had changed tactics. They began pounding the British capital with high explosive bombs, trying to force Churchill and his government to beg for peace. Months of deadly night raids followed and people quickly named this new ordeal *the Blitz.*

Taking shelter

After the first raid, thousands of civilians streamed out of the city, looking for safety in the countryside or with relatives in distant towns. But most stayed behind, reluctant to abandon their friends, families and jobs. The attacks began with sirens wailing across the rooftops to warn of raiders approaching. Wardens helped people into public shelters – brick and concrete huts that offered some protection from the bombs. But, as the planes circled overhead, everyone on the ground knew there was little chance of surviving a direct hit.

Desperate to escape the noise and danger of the raids, up to 177,000 Londoners took to sleeping on the platforms of the city's underground railway stations. As the Blitz continued, local councils organized beds, medical care, and even mobile libraries and entertainers, to make life more bearable in these subterranean shelters.

Business as usual

Despite all the dangers and disruption, most Londoners managed to get on with their lives. People went to work – walking, if necessary – along the shattered roads. Shops and restaurants stayed open, even when all their windows had been blown out. "More open than usual" was the cheeky sign left outside some blitzed shops.

The fighting spirit of London was never broken, something Churchill and the national newspapers were quick to point out. But in diaries and private conversations, many people confessed their worries. How long would the Blitz last, and how much more could London take?

St. Paul's Cathedral stands alone in an ocean of fire, in this photo taken from the rooftops at the height of an air raid on December 29, 1940.

With no fighters to protect them at night, blitzed cities relied on spotlights to trace the skies for enemy bombers, and anti-aircraft, or 'ack-ack' guns, to shoot them down.

Barrage balloons floated on heavy steel cables. These cables were designed to snag any low-flying enemy aircraft. London had a protective canopy of over 400 balloons.

Later in the war, the RAF fitted radar sets to their fighter planes to track night bombers. Desperate to keep their invention a secret, they told journalists that British pilots ate lots of carrots, and this helped them to see in the dark.

The Coventry inferno

Although London bore the brunt of the Blitz, the shadow of German bombers fell across dozens of other British towns and cities. Ports and industrial zones were raided, from Edinburgh and Belfast to Portsmouth, and thousands of civilians living close to military targets were killed or maimed. But the air war took a new and horrific turn in November 1940, when the *Luftwaffe* raided Coventry and burned it to the ground.

Coventry was a major target because its factories were vital to the British war effort. But RAF fighters couldn't protect the city from a night attack. At this stage in the war, pilots still relied on their eyesight to find and intercept enemy planes. Flying at high altitudes and hiding in the dark, enemy bombers were almost impossible to spot.

Firestorm

The first wave of *Luftwaffe* raiders arrived directly over Coventry and dropped thousands of small incendiary bombs – metal tubes packed with burning chemicals. As the main force of 400 bombers approached their target, the Germans could see the city from 240km (150 miles) away, covered in giant flames.

High explosive bombs demolished buildings and spread burning materials across the city. The fires grew so hot they melted bricks and sucked the air out of underground shelters. Over 500 people were killed, cremated or buried alive in the firestorm.

The next morning, the 'All Clear' sirens sounded at last. The survivors clambered out of their air raid shelters into a smoking, hellish landscape of twisted steel and rubble. Even their stately cathedral had been reduced to a charred ruin.

Recovery and retaliation

Such was the extent of the destruction in the city, that a new term was coined: 'coventrated' – meaning flattened by bombing. But, amazingly, Coventry recovered from the attack. Although the *Luftwaffe* claimed the raid a success, many factories reopened within six weeks, and people built new homes. Later in the war, as a reprisal for Coventry and other cities blitzed in 1940 and 41, the RAF launched a series of devastating air raids on German towns and cities, killing a shocking estimated total of 650,000 civilians.

Peace beacon

In recent years, Coventry – with its new cathedral – has become a symbol for the suffering experienced by civilians in wartime. The city hosts an annual conference devoted to peace and understanding between nations.

Winston Churchill walks through the devastated ruins of Coventry Cathedral.

A pack of seven German U-boats sets out to sea to hunt down and destroy Allied convoys.

The Germans called the U-boat tactic of hunting merchant ships in large groups *Rudeltaktik*, or pack tactic, so these gangs of U-boats were nicknamed 'wolf packs'.

Posters, such as this one, warned people not to say anything in public that might give away the routes of convoy ships to German spies.

Beating the wolf packs

Britain's vast fleet of cargo ships was its lifeline to the outside world. The merchant navy supplied two thirds of the country's food and brought precious guns, fuel and steel from America. But German submarines, or U-boats, lurked in the wastes of the sea, sinking hundreds of ships with their torpedoes. The British had to keep the ocean highways open, or they would quickly lose the war.

Sea hunters

The Royal Navy had beaten the U-boats in the First World War by using the 'convoy' system. Cargo ships crossed the Atlantic Ocean in large groups, or convoys, protected by armed merchant ships. Royal Navy warships only joined them when they entered the dangerous waters close to home. But in 1940, from their new bases in occupied France, U-boats could hunt deep in the heart of the Atlantic, for convoys that had no warship escorts.

After spotting a convoy, U-boat captains tracked it for days, sending radio messages to other submarines. They waited until a 'wolf pack' of six or more U-boats assembled, before surfacing and attacking under cover of darkness. Raids could stretch over several nights and some convoys lost as many as half of their ships.

24

The longest battle

The Battle of the Atlantic, as Churchill named it, turned into a desperate struggle which lasted until the end of the war – although the worst was over by May 1943. Although merchant sailors were civilians, they took the same risks as soldiers. Around 30,000 of them died at sea, while the U-boats and Allied navies wrestled for control of the waves.

Search and destroy

Churchill understood that his first task was to protect the convoys. In September 1940, he signed an agreement with the United States, who gave him 50 old destroyer warships. The Royal Navy had also been busy building a new fleet of small escort vessels. Soon every convoy had a warship escort right across the Atlantic.

These new escorts were fitted with special weapons for detecting and destroying U-boats. Radar picked them up on the surface, and sonar equipment used sound waves to locate them underwater. Destroyers and other vessels chased after any U-boats, attacking them with drums of explosives called depth charges.

Britain was fighting back, but the Battle of the Atlantic was far from over. It intensified in 1941, when the Germans sent their most powerful warship, *Bismarck*, to help their U-boats smash the convoys.

Chasing echoes

Sonar was used to hunt submarines. It works in a similar way to radar, except it uses sound instead of radio waves.

The submarine hunter sends out pulses of sound, in a cone shape, under the water.

When sound bounces off the submarine, the hunter hears an echo in his headphones. He follows the echo to locate the submarine.

As the hunter passes over the submarine, it attacks, dropping depth charges.

Home Front fighters

Bombed in their cities and under siege at sea, the British people quickly adapted to life in a war zone. Getting about, shopping and working became a daily struggle, and old habits and attitudes had to change. As men were drafted into the army, millions of women took up new jobs to keep the country fighting.

A ration book contained coupons to be exchanged for rations. One person's rations for a week were:

· A few slices of bacon or ham and one portion of other meat

· A tub of butter, a small piece of cheese, one egg and two or three pints of milk

Tightening the belt

To make the best use of Britain's food supplies, the government brought in rationing in January 1940. Everyone received a ration book that listed how much sugar, bacon and butter they were allowed to buy each week. Shopkeepers had to check and stamp these books before selling any goods.

Even with rationing in force there were shortages. Shoppers had to wait in long lines outside each store, hoping the shelves wouldn't be empty when they got inside. Not everyone played by the rules. Small time crooks, known as spivs, supplied luxuries like chocolate and silk stockings to anyone who could afford them.

Making do

By 1943 most foods were either rationed or difficult to find in the shops, and fuel, paper, soap and clothing had been added to the list. But, despite the shortages, people found ways of 'making do' with what they had.

The government issued recipe books to help people to make the most of their rations. These included cake mixtures made with powdered eggs...

...and fudge made with carrots.

People were urged to repair and recycle their old clothes.

With nylon stockings in short supply, some girls painted fake seams onto their legs.

The stronger sex

Many women had little time for food shopping. They were just too busy working long shifts in Britain's growing armaments industry. At the height of the war, a third of all factory workers were female. Young mothers helped build planes and tanks, as other women set up nurseries to care for their children. Every woman aged between 18 and 50 was 'called up' for some kind of war service. Thousands worked as wardens, ambulance drivers and fire spotters. Others joined the armed forces, where they were expected to do everything a man would do, except go into combat.

On the farm

Even in the quiet of the countryside, the old way of life was changing. By 1944, tens of thousands of women toiled in the fields as part of the Women's Land Army, helping farmers plant and harvest their crops. They were known as 'Land Girls' – although many of them had never been out of the city before.

Grow your own

To supplement food rations, the Ministry of Food launched a 'Dig For Victory' campaign, to get people gardening.

Parks, tennis courts and flowerbeds were dug up and planted over with vegetables, as everyone tried to grow extra food for the table.

The government also encouraged clubs of friends or co-workers to keep pigs and chickens.

By the end of the war, Britain had halved the amount of food it imported by sea.

These Land Girls are making hay while the sun shines.

The Home Guard

As you were

Men with vital jobs, known as 'reserved occupations' were not allowed to go into the armed forces, but they could still serve in the Home Guard.

Butchers, dentists, schoolteachers and lighthouse keepers all had to stay at their jobs throughout the war.

Lots of British men were too young or too old to serve in the regular forces, but they still wanted to fight if there was an invasion. In May 1940, the government asked for male volunteers to join a new defence force. Over a million signed up – from teenage boys to retired generals. This became known as the Home Guard.

But the British army was struggling to rearm itself after Dunkirk and there were no spare weapons for Home Guard units. So volunteers carried pitchforks, old shotguns and swords until they received better equipment. Almost half the men were veteran fighters from the First World War and what they lacked in equipment they made up for in enthusiasm. They were a reassuring sight for the public, patrolling the countryside and capturing crashed German airmen.

This teenage Home Guard volunteer is being trained to use a 'Tommy' gun.

These Bevin Boys are on their way to work down the coal mines in Pontefract, Yorkshire.

In the pits

Call-up papers arrived in the post, ordering men to report to their local barracks for training. But some young recruits were handed a shovel instead of a gun – and sent to dig coal in Britain's mines. Too many coal miners had enlisted and the Minister of Labour, Ernest Bevin, needed almost 50,000 extra men to strengthen the workforce. Many of these new recruits, who became known as Bevin Boys, were shocked by the miner's hard, dangerous life underground.

Coal was in short supply for years after the war, and some Bevin Boys weren't released from duty in the mines until 1948.

Even members of the Royal Family had to 'do their bit' – Princess Elizabeth, the future Queen, trained as a mechanic.

Mixing and mingling

Rationing, war work and the blackout made life a struggle on the Home Front, but most people pulled together and shared the hardships. As young men and women went into new jobs in new places, they had a chance to see how others lived. Some were surprised by the poverty and poor living conditions they came across. In the grip of war, Britain was discovering itself, and learning lessons for the future.

29

Children in Liverpool station, waiting to be evacuated to the countryside

War kids

The war years were the best and worst of times for Britain's children. Of the millions evacuated to the country, some loved their new homes, while others were homesick and miserable. In the cities, children lived in fear of air raids, but it was exciting to be in the thick of the action. Despite all its terrors and upheavals, growing up during the war was an incredible adventure.

Choose me

Children who were being evacuated usually went by train, leaving in small groups from their schools. Each child had a name label pinned to their clothes, and the lucky ones received a ration of chocolate for the journey. After arriving in country villages and towns, the evacuees met local people who had offered to take them in. Some children were herded together, while adults looked them up and down as though they were choosing a new pet. Waiting to be chosen was a heartbreaking experience for many evacuees.

Evacuees

People taking evacuees received cash from the government and could shop with their ration books. So some foster parents may have been more interested in the extra rations than in the children.

Some evacuees had never left their cities before and were amazed when they saw cows and sheep for the first time.

Hard times

Country people were often shocked to discover lice and other vermin living on their new guests. Lots of the evacuees came from slum areas in the cities, where poverty and housing conditions were far worse than they are today. Houses with bathrooms and running hot water were rare, and most city kids had only one good clean a week – in council wash houses or public baths.

Sandbag scholars

Even in the worst days of the Blitz there was no escape from school. When the air raid sirens began to howl, children rushed to public shelters or to schoolrooms that had been strengthened with sandbags and steel girders. Pupils who lived nearby and had an Anderson shelter in the garden were allowed to run home.

Dangerous games

Air raids provided the material for a new kind of treasure hunting – collecting shrapnel. Children scoured bomb sites for bits of twisted steel from exploded bombs, and then traded them in the playground.

   Aircraft spotting was another pastime, and city kids soon learned how to identify enemy planes from the noise of their engines.

   Later in the war, American soldiers arrived with exciting treats – chewing gum, chocolate and comics.

Playing in the rubble of their bombed city street, these boys have rigged up a makeshift swing from a broken lamp post.

The secret war

While Britain's armed forces licked their wounds after Dunkirk, Churchill assembled a secret army of spies, scientists and elite soldiers. His special agents and intelligence experts launched raids into occupied Europe and helped make one of the most important breakthroughs of the war – cracking the top-secret code that the Germans used to send their radio messages.

Special forces

Churchill told his commanders he wanted to "set Europe ablaze" with sudden attacks and sabotage missions. The army asked its best soldiers to volunteer for a new fighting unit to carry out these raids, known as the Commandos. Volunteers had to undergo a gruelling training course in special combat skills, deep in the forests of the Scottish Highlands.

Commando troops learned how to use small boats and parachute drops to strike into enemy territory. Their missions were secret – and often fatal – as German soldiers had orders to shoot any commandos they captured.

X-men

Despite the dangers, there were still lots of volunteers, including hundreds of Jewish refugees from Nazi-occupied Europe. Some of these men were wanted by the German secret police, the *Gestapo*, and their unit was so secret, it was known only as X-troop.

This photograph shows a commando abseiling down a sheer cliff, during a training exercise.

Commando training also included long hikes through snow and rain, after which commandos had to drag themselves over a forest assault course of rope swings, ditches and high fences, while grenades and machine guns went off all around them.

Double-dealings

Britain used its spies inside Europe to watch German troop movements and smuggle crashed Allied airmen back to safety. Other agents pretended to be working for the enemy, but passed them false information. These 'double agents' wasted the German's time and resources, and tricked them about the true locations of planned operations.

The British army didn't send women into combat, but Churchill decided that an exception should be made with its special agents. Dozens of women parachuted into occupied France to help local Resistance groups fighting the Germans. It was dangerous work: many agents of both sexes were caught by the *Gestapo* and murdered or sent to prison camps.

Spy gadgets

Agents needed special equipment for missions into enemy territory. They carried forged identity papers, portable radios and explosives.

British scientists made fake logs, hollowed out to hide weapons in. They designed special toothpaste tubes for sneaking in coded messages and they even developed a 'dead rat' bomb!

Cracking the code

The war's most amazing spying success took place far from any battlefield, in a quiet country house in southern England. A group of British and Allied scientists, maths experts and spies had gathered at Bletchley Park, to make sense of the German military's radio messages. The Germans had devised a typewriter-sized machine called Enigma to scramble their messages into an unreadable code.

Building on the work already done by Polish mathematicians, the Bletchley Park team began to unpick Enigma. They built a machine that could quickly run through millions of calculations – an early version of a computer – and by 1940 they were decoding the German messages. The Enigma triumph saved thousands of lives and helped the Allies win the war.

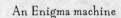
An Enigma machine

33

Hunting Bismarck

Big guns

Bismarck's guns fired shells as big as a man, weighing as much as a car. They had a long range, too. The shell that sank the *Hood* was fired at a distance of 14.5km (9 miles) away.

This photograph shows the German battleship *Bismarck* in 1941, shortly before the ship was sent into combat.

Towering over the waves, warships displayed the raw power of fighting nations. The massive HMS *Hood* was a floating fortress and the pride of the British fleet. When Germany's fearsome battleship, *Bismarck*, set out to raid the Atlantic convoys, the Royal Navy sent a task force led by *Hood* to stop her.

Launched in 1918, *Hood* was old for a warship, but still packed a deadly punch with eight huge guns. The ship was longer than two soccer pitches, and was famed and feared around the world. But *Hood* had a fatal flaw: the steel plates protecting her decks were vulnerable to shells falling from above. In contrast, *Bismarck* was a state-of-the-art killing machine, with better gun accuracy and defensive protection. Even so, most British sailors thought *Hood* was unbeatable.

Bismarck and a smaller warship, *Prinz Eugen*, tried to sneak into the Atlantic Ocean through the Denmark Straits – the channel between Greenland and Iceland. But, early in the morning of May 24, 1941, *Hood* and another Royal Navy battleship, HMS *Prince of Wales* intercepted them. The British fired first, heading towards the enemy at top speed.

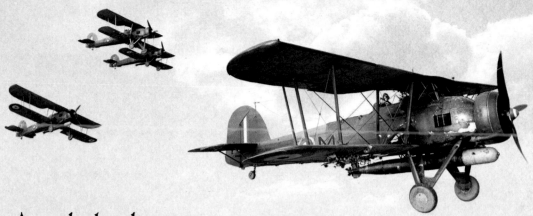

An unlucky shot

Only minutes later, a plunging shell from *Bismarck* smashed through *Hood's* deck and exploded inside the magazine, where all the ship's munitions are stored. Sailors on the *Prince of Wales* stared in horror, as *Hood* was torn apart by a huge blast. The Royal Navy's strongest ship lurched into the air and vanished below the sea. *Hood* sank so quickly, that only three of the 1,418 crew survived.

Alone, outgunned and badly damaged, the *Prince of Wales* broke off the attack, granting victory to the Germans. The battle shocked the Allies, and was a triumph for Hitler. But celebrations on board the *Bismarck* were short-lived. A British shell had flooded the ship's fuel tanks, and her captain decided to run for a safe port in France to make repairs. He never made it.

Out for revenge

Desperate to avenge the loss of *Hood*, the Royal Navy sent every ship it could muster to chase the *Bismarck*. An attack by Swordfish planes dropping torpedoes struck the first blow, wrecking the German battleship's rudder. Unable to steer, the *Bismarck* wheeled around in a huge circle, while British warships closed in for the kill. After two hours of heavy shelling and torpedo attacks, *Bismarck* joined *Hood* on the bottom of the sea.

Lumbering through the air with its heavy torpedo attached underneath, the Fairey Swordfish was comical to look at. But these planes could sink ships and became essential to the war at sea.

Fight to the last

Under British fire, a German admiral on the *Bismarck* knew he was beaten, but sent a message saying, "Ship incapable of manoeuvring. Will fight to the last shell. Long live the Fuhrer!"

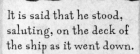

It is said that he stood, saluting, on the deck of the ship as it went down.

New allies, new enemies

By May 1941, the Blitz was over. German bombs had killed more than 40,000 civilians and pulverized towns, factories and homes, but Britain was still unbeaten. For almost a year, the country had been under siege and fighting alone. Now the war was spreading, and the most powerful nations on earth would be forced to take sides.

Uncle Joe

The *Luftwaffe* broke off their attacks on Britain to support a new invasion – into the Soviet Union. For years, Hitler had dreamed of capturing its fertile lands and oil fields. In June he unleashed an army of three million men to bring the country to its knees. Many of these soldiers never came home.

Hitler was a ruthless tyrant with a passion for war, but he had met his match in Stalin. A cunning, brutal man, Stalin expected his soldiers to fight to the death. Over the coming years, 24 million Russians (military and civilians) died, as Stalin steadily annihilated Hitler's army. Although Churchill was deeply suspicious of Stalin and his intentions in Europe, he welcomed him as a vital ally.

A day of terror

Many Americans wanted no part in the war. But, on December 7, 1941, a new enemy stunned the United States with a sneak attack on American battleships in the Pacific. Japan had entered the war.

Like Germany, Japan was hungry for new territories and the two countries were already political allies. But Japanese naval commanders feared the power of the American fleet moored at Pearl Harbor, Hawaii. In a dawn attack, hundreds of Japanese dive bombers and torpedo planes mauled the US fleet, sinking several battleships and killing more than 2,000 sailors.

The Americans were outraged, and US congress declared war on Japan the following day. But even as the British celebrated gaining a strong new ally, Japanese troops were storming Britain's colonies in the Far East.

Posters like this one persuaded thousands of American men to join the armed forces to defend their nation.

A US warship explodes during the Japanese raid on Pearl Harbor, December 7, 1941. US President Roosevelt described it as "a date which will live in infamy."

Japanese troops march
in to occupy the British
colonial city of Singapore.

Disaster in the East

The military base at Singapore was a cornerstone of the British empire, standing guard over Britain's territories across South East Asia. With almost 100,000 troops and two large warships at his disposal, the base commander, General Percival, thought he could smash any enemy attack. But he was soon proved wrong.

Gunboat diplomacy

Japan had been at war with China since 1937, and desperately needed the rich reserves of rubber, metals and oil found in Britain's eastern colonies and the Dutch East Indies. Within hours of the Pearl Harbor raid on Decmber 7, 1941, Japanese troops landed in Malaya, 800km (500 miles) north of Singapore. The British sent their two warships to intercept the enemy's fleet. But the Japanese, using dive bombers and torpedo planes, sank both British ships on December 10.

South East Asia

The red shading on this map shows areas under Japanese occupation by 1942.

CHINA

BURMA

Hong Kong

THAILAND

FRENCH INDOCHINA

MALAYA

Singapore

BORNEO

SUMATRA

DUTCH EAST INDIES

38

Singapore falls

Many British officers thought their men — including troops from New Zealand, Australia, and India — were fitter and braver than their attackers. But Japan's soldiers were battle-hard after years of savage combat in China and fought their way down to Singapore by the end of January. On February 15, the British were forced to surrender the base. It was a humiliating defeat. Churchill's forces were broken in the East, and countries as far away as India, New Zealand and Australia were now under threat of invasion.

A green hell

After the surrender, Percival and over 80,000 of his men became POWs — prisoners of war — and many were sent to camps in the jungle. The Japanese treatment of their prisoners was one of the worst atrocities of the war. POWs were beaten, starved and worked to death building roads and train lines for their captors. Their ordeal would last until the war ended, three long years later.

This is a sketch by Ronald Searle, a British artist who was a Japanese POW.

It shows emaciated prisoners cutting into a mountain with hammers and chisels, and hauling rocks to make way for a new train line from Thailand to Burma.

Bicycle blitzkrieg

Many of Japan's soldiers advanced through Malaya using bicycles to speed their progress along narrow jungle tracks.

The savagery of the Japanese soldiers horrified the British. Thousands of local civilians, especially those of Chinese origin, were murdered.

As well as the military prisoners, the Japanese rounded up and imprisoned some 130,000 Allied civilians who had been living in the region.

Duel in the desert

Some of Britain's earliest, and most spectacular victories of the Second World War were won in the deserts of North Africa. The stakes were high. Churchill's army in Egypt had to protect the Suez Canal and the oilfields in Iraq and Iran that powered Britain's tanks and factories. After a series of breathtaking tank battles, the British commander, Bernard Montgomery, emerged as a national hero.

'The Full Monty'

Montgomery liked to stand out from the crowd. He always wore his trademark black beret for photographers. More at ease in the company of ordinary soldiers than generals, his men adored him.

 Some people think the term 'the Full Monty' came from Monty's habit of always eating huge, cooked breakfasts with all the trimmings – even in the desert.

The fox arrives

The British had been fighting in the desert since 1940, when they had smashed the Italian forces in Libya. Italy was Hitler's major ally – alongside Japan – among the Axis Powers. Hitler sent a daredevil tank commander, Erwin Rommel, to help the Italians. A brilliant and cunning general, Rommel soon earned himself the nickname, the 'Desert Fox'. His *Afrika Korps* soldiers quickly outfought and outflanked the British army, pushing it back into Egypt.

A British tank raises clouds of dust and sand as the Allies storm through the desert during the Battle of El Alamein.

Territory mostly held by Nazi-occupied France

Axis occupation

Allied occupation

ALGERIA

TUNISIA

Mediterranean Sea

MOROCCO

Suez Canal

Battlefields of North Africa, 1940-1942

El Alamein

Cairo

LIBYA

EGYPT

Under a burning sun

Allied soldiers rested in Cairo, drinking and socializing, before setting out into the pitiless heat of the desert battlefields. Water, food and ammunition were always in short supply, and sudden sandstorms could blow up, trapping men inside their vehicles for days.

By July 1942, Rommel's men were within striking distance of Cairo. The British dug in at the coastal town of El Alamein, blocking the approaches to Cairo with trenches and minefields. In August, a new commander took charge – Montgomery, or 'Monty' as soldiers called him. Monty had studied Rommel's tactics and secretly stockpiled huge numbers of guns and vehicles. In October he pierced Rommel's line, using air strikes and artillery to clear the way for his tanks.

Monty's triumph

Rommel's army scrambled back to Libya, losing thousands of men, tanks and trucks. Monty had beaten one of Germany's best generals and became a celebrity across the Allied nations. The Axis troops in North Africa surrendered in May 1943, and the Desert Fox slipped away to Germany. Only a year later, he would face Monty in the battlefields of Normandy.

Time out

At rest in Cairo, Allied soldiers had a chance to see the pyramids or catch a movie. There were also shows by entertainers, such as George Formby, who went out to keep up the morale of the troops.

Lots of soldiers who fought in the desert described it as a gentlemanly war. In some battles, soldiers arranged an afternoon truce, so that the British could 'brew-up' – make tea – and let the Germans drink coffee.

Bouncing bombs

Barnes Wallis (on the left) and four British officials watch as his bouncing bomb – codenamed 'Upkeep' – bounces along the water during a trial run.

Britain's scientists and designers were world class and they worked feverishly to develop winning tools for the armed forces. Their radar and code-breaking computer were dazzling achievements, but perhaps the most ingenious British invention of the war was a bomb that could bounce across water.

Thirsty work

'Boffin' was a cheeky term for the brilliant – but absent-minded – scientists who assisted the British military.

A boffin known only as 'Q' features in the James Bond stories by Ian Fleming. The writer had served with the Royal Naval Intelligence Division services during the war.

Some of Hitler's most important weapons factories were located in the Ruhr region of Germany. These factories relied on several, massive dams in the area for power and water. RAF commanders wanted to blast the dams and wreck the factories, but bombs dropped from above didn't have enough explosive power to break the thick dam walls. The Germans had even hung underwater nets across the reservoirs to stop torpedo plane attacks.

It was a British aircraft designer, Barnes Wallis, who came up with the breathtaking solution for blowing up the dams. Wallis believed that an underwater bomb, placed next to the dam wall, would have enough power to breach it.

Marbles

Instead of dropping the bomb from above, Wallis suggested *bouncing* it across the reservoir like a spinning stone. The bomb would hit the dam and sink, hugging the wall before exploding. The RAF thought Wallis was crazy.

But instead of giving up, Wallis decided to prove that his idea was possible. With the help of his children, he conducted experiments with a bucket of water, some marbles and a catapult. These tests helped Wallis to calculate the exact height and speed of the bombing attack. He then persuaded the RAF to build a dummy bomb and drop it from one of their planes. The bomb bounced, and the RAF began planning a raid.

Not all wartime science was destructive. In 1944, Allied chemists helped to save the lives of thousands of soldiers and civilians by developing a new infection-killing drug – penicillin.

The Dambusters

In May 1943, 19 Lancaster bombers flew deep into Germany. Their bouncing bombs destroyed two dams, flooding miles of open country and disrupting the work going on in the Hitler's factories. The raid was a success, but it came at a terrible price. Wallis wept when he learned that eight of the bomber crews – who became known as the 'Dambusters' – had been killed or shot down during the attack.

Water floods through the breach in the Mohne Dam, four hours after the Dambusters' raid in May 1943.

The road to Rome

American commanders had always believed that the quickest way to defeat Hitler was to strike at him through France. After victory in North Africa, they wanted to invade as soon as possible, but Churchill persuaded Roosevelt that the Allies should first attack the weak underbelly of the Axis – in Italy.

Major Martin

The island of Sicily was only a short sea crossing from Allied bases in Tunisia. From Sicily, Allied soldiers could stream into southern Italy and capture Rome. Italian and German troops were expecting an attack. But British secret agents came up with an amazing bluff to put them off their guard.

In April 1943, German spies got hold of the body of a British man, Major Martin, found floating at sea. With him were plans for an invasion of Greece and Sardinia. Hitler moved guns and troops to these locations, instead of Sicily. But the mystery major was a decoy and the plans were fakes.

Snail's pace

This German poster pokes fun at the slow progress the Allies made from Sicily, at the southern tip of Italy, to Rome.

Italy is a narrow, mountainous country, which made it easy to defend, but difficult for the Allies to attack.

The sinking ship

In July, Allied troops made a landing on Sicily. With enemy troops inside his country's borders, the Italian king decided it was foolish to support Hitler. So he sacked Mussolini and surrendered to the Allies. Hitler sent paratroopers to rescue his old friend, but by then, Mussolini was a broken man. Germany's main ally in Europe was out of the war.

Bomb proof

Allied troops celebrated when they heard that the Italians had put down their weapons, but the fighting in Italy dragged on. By the spring of 1944, they were locked in a ferocious struggle with German defenders south of Rome. The Germans occupied a mountain monastery – Monte Cassino – which blocked the Allied advance. Even after a massive bombing raid, the monastery's foundations stood firm. It took the Allies four months of vicious fighting to capture this cliff top fortress. But on June 4, they finally reached Rome and freed the city from the Germans.

Sunny Italy

The Italian campaign never received the same newspaper attention as the invasion of France (D-Day) and many British soldiers thought they were mocked at home for taking a holiday in sunny Italy.

We're the D-Day Dodgers, way out in Italy, Always on the vino, always on the spree...

Veterans of Monte Cassino made up this song after a joke went around that they were D-Day Dodgers.

After heavy fighting in the mountains, these are the shattered remains of the grand, historic monastery at Monte Cassino.

Tonic for the troops

The war was a strange and unsettling experience for millions of Allied soldiers, scattered around the globe. Most of them had never been away from their friends and families before, and when they weren't fighting they suffered from boredom and homesickness. A visit from a movie star or famous singer was a welcome relief from the terrors of war.

Home entertainment

Soldiers decorated their quarters with postcards or pin-up photographs of movie starlets taken from magazines. There were no televisions, but the troops had radios and movie projectors and could watch news bulletins and cartoons. British units formed their own concert parties made up of any singers, comedians and musicians from among their ranks. They staged shows and sketches and many of them, like Peter Sellers and Spike Milligan, went on to become stars after the war.

NOEL COWARD'S
"IN WHICH WE SERVE"
A TWO CITIES FILM

NOEL COWARD · JOHN MILLS
BERNARD MILES · CELIA JOHNSON
JOYCE CAREY · KAY WALSH

This is a poster for a 1942 movie, written by and starring Noël Coward. The movie told the heroic story of a ship's crew that took part in the Dunkirk evacuation. It was a big hit, and won an Academy Award.

In this photograph, British sailors are crowded on the deck of HMS *Nelson* to watch Phyllis Stanley perform.

Forces' Sweetheart Vera Lynn receives a grand welcome from some of her sailor fans as she arrives to put on a show for British troops.

In addition to her concert performances, Vera Lynn also had her own radio show in which she sang and read out messages from those separated by the conflict.

Sweethearts and swingers

Visiting starlets were more popular than amateur entertainers. Probably the most popular was a British singer, Vera Lynn, known as the Forces' Sweetheart. She performed concerts for Allied troops across Egypt, India and Burma. Lynn wanted British soldiers to know that the people at home had not forgotten them. Her 1939 song, 'We'll Meet Again' became an anthem for troops and civilians all around the world.

American troops introduced their own brand of entertainment to the Brits. Among the most popular American performers were a cheeky British-born comedian named Bob Hope, and Major Glenn Miller, a musician. Miller had joined the US forces in 1942, to set up a touring band playing swing jazz. In 1944, he brought his band to England to play for the thousands of American soldiers in training there.

But, entertaining in a war zone could be a dangerous business. In December 1944, Miller's plane disappeared without a trace during a flight to Paris.

Wartime anthems

Here are some lyrics from two of Vera Lynn's most popular wartime songs:

"We'll meet again,
don't know where,
don't know when,
But I know we'll meet
again, some sunny day."

From 'We'll Meet Again'

"There'll be blue birds over
The white cliffs of Dover,
Tomorrow, just you
wait and see.
There'll be love
and laughter
And peace ever after
Tomorrow, when the
world is free."

From 'The White
Cliffs of Dover'

A day to remember

On June 6, 1944, British and Allied forces launched the largest sea invasion the world had ever seen. Against all odds, they landed an army on the beaches of Normandy, France and began a long and bloody advance on Germany that would end the war.

Breaking the wall

The Germans were expecting the Allies and had been busy fortifying the European coast from Norway to Spain with minefields, machine gun posts and concrete watchtowers. Hitler called this defensive line his Atlantic Wall and gave Field Marshal Rommel the job of holding it against all attacks. Rommel was a bold commander, and promised Hitler that his tanks would push any invading army back into the sea.

Operation Overlord

The Atlantic Wall was a tough nut to crack, but the Allies were desperate to open a new battlefront in France. This was the most direct route into Germany, and for months Stalin had been demanding that Allied troops take the pressure off his exhausted army, fighting in the East. Using the codename *Overlord*, British and American officers began planning a massive military strike into occupied France.

This is a photograph of the Sherman floating tank. In the water, the screen around the tank was raised to make it float and propellers at the rear drove it forward.

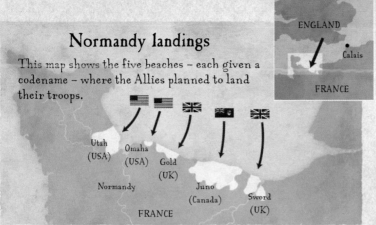

Normandy landings

This map shows the five beaches – each given a codename – where the Allies planned to land their troops.

ENGLAND

Calais

FRANCE

Utah (USA)

Omaha (USA)

Gold (UK)

Normandy

Juno (Canada)

Sword (UK)

FRANCE

Landing places

While they prepared for the attack, the Allies assembled a fake invasion force on the English coast across from Calais. This convinced Rommel that they were heading there instead.

Most troops would get to Normandy by sea, on flat-bottomed landing craft, but others would arrive by parachute or glider.

Plan of attack

Overlord called for an armada of ships to carry more than one million fighting men – and all their equipment – across the English Channel to Normandy. Arriving at dawn, Allied warships would pound the coast with massive shells, while a fleet of small landing craft ferried the troops to shore. Crack soldiers and special tanks would smash through any German opposition, pushing miles inland before stopping for the night.

Storm warning

America's General Dwight Eisenhower was the Allies' overall commander of the operation, with Montgomery in charge of the ground troops. Both agreed that June 5 was the best date for D-Day – the day of the attack – because of good weather and tide forecasts. But, on the evening of June 4, a storm was brewing. Thousands of men had already boarded their ships, weighed down with weapons and supplies. They waited in port until a British weather expert predicted clear skies for the morning of June 6 and Eisenhower gave the order to go.

There were no safe ports in Normandy – so the Allies built their own floating concrete docks, called Mulberries. These would be towed across the English Channel to receive supplies.

Red devils

The Germans called British paratroopers 'Red devils' – in a tribute to their courage and the maroon beret they wore into battle.

On the beaches

The first Allied soldiers to land in France were British and American paratroopers, with orders to capture vital bridges and roads ahead of the main attack. Although some paratroopers dropped miles from their targets, they soon spread panic and confusion among the German defenders.

The beach landings began just after dawn. Hundreds of Allied troops drowned in the surf, or were machine-gunned as they struggled on the sand. The most savage fighting was at Omaha Beach, where the Americans landed. At one stage it looked as though the attackers might be beaten back, but the Americans rallied and broke through the German lines. By nightfall, all five beaches were under Allied control.

British commandos rush off their flat-bottomed landing craft onto the beach at Normandy on D-Day.

A new front

Despite the hard fighting, D-Day ended in a total victory for the Allies. By the end of June, they had landed 850,000 men and 150,000 vehicles. Allied planes ruled the skies over Normandy, their bombers blasting German tanks and trucks with rockets, miles behind enemy lines. British commandos and paratroopers had fought deep into German occupied territory, and all Rommel's efforts to counter-attack with his elite tank divisions were defeated.

Since 1940, Churchill had supported the French General Charles de Gaulle in building French forces outside France. Known as the Free French, they played a key role in driving out the Germans from France. Fighting was tough, but by the end of August, the Allies had liberated Paris and begun their long march to Berlin.

Bravery beyond the call of duty

It was the courage of ordinary soldiers, like Stanley Hollis, that gave the Allies victory on D-Day. Arriving on Gold beach, Hollis rushed two enemy machine guns and captured dozens of Germans.

Later in the day, he risked his life again when he rescued some friends under fire.

Hollis won the Victoria Cross – Britain's highest award for bravery.

This is a German V-1 flying bomb being launched. Powered in the sky by a jet engine, the bomb was usually launched from a ramp, using a catapult.

'Bomber' Harris

The Germans weren't the only ones to blitz enemy cities. Under the command of Sir Arthur Harris – nicknamed 'Bomber' Harris– the RAF, along with the US Air Force, carried out a number of bombing raids on German cities.

Cologne, May 1942: 469 killed and 450,000 left homeless

Hamburg, July 1943: 42,000 civilians killed

Dresden, February 1945: hundreds of historic buildings destroyed, and an estimated 25,000-35,000 people killed

Rocket blitz

The triumph of D-Day gave the British public their first real hopes for a quick end to the war. For almost four years they had endured air raids, hunger and hard work, and the misery of the blackout. But while they celebrated, a nightmarish new weapon was aimed against them – the German rocket bomb.

Flying bombs

In mid-June 1944, small, pilotless planes with explosive warheads began crashing into London and the south coast of England. These were the first of Hitler's vengeance weapons – known as V-1s – designed to slaughter civilians. Powered by crude jet engines, V-1s were launched from bases across Nazi occupied France and Holland and more than 2,000 crashed into the British capital.

Watching and waiting

The flying bombs had a terrifying impact on Londoners. Many V-1s arrived in the daytime, when everyone was out of the shelters and the streets were busy. Their engines made a rumbling growl as they sliced across the sky, but when the noise suddenly stopped, people ran for their lives. This was the signal that the bomb would dive to earth, and hundreds might die.

Closing the gap

In the early attacks, most V-1s reached London and southern England. But the RAF soon developed tactics for destroying the flying bombs. Radar stations tracked them as they crossed the English Channel, sending radio warnings to fighter pilots who intercepted the bombs. By late August, the RAF was stopping almost every V-1. Just weeks later the raids ended, when Allied troops captured the launching sites.

Silent killer

The next vengeance weapon seemed unstoppable. In September, a massive blast ripped through West London and the city was soon hit by dozens of mystery explosions. German scientists had unleashed a new weapon – the V-2. It was an early version of the space rocket that flew faster than the speed of sound. Hitler boasted that the V-2 would win him the war, but his rocket was so expensive and difficult to make, only a few thousand were launched before Germany lay in ruins.

Tipping point

RAF pilots discovered a dangerous trick for destroying V-1s – even when their guns had run out of ammunition.

They flew next to the weapon and slowly raised their wingtip, until it was only inches from the bomb's wing. The turbulence from the fighter's wing flipped the V-1 over and it crashed to the ground, safely away from any highly-populated areas.

A V-2 rocket is launched by British scientists, after it was abandoned by retreating Nazis.

Horror at Belsen

Some Jews escaped the terrors of the death camps. Thousands tried to leave Germany before the war, but foreign governments were often reluctant to give them sanctuary.

In November 1938, Nazi thugs ransacked Jewish homes and businesses. The violence spurred Britain's government into action. They offered shelter to any Jewish children under the age of seventeen. Around 10,000 girls and boys made the desperate journey across Europe by train and boat, as part of the *Kindertransport* – moving the children.

Hitler closed Germany's borders when the war started and most of the newcomers never saw their parents again.

Many joined Britain's armed forces as soon as they were old enough, and fought bravely to defeat the evil that had driven them from their homes.

Many soldiers have moments of panic on the battlefield, when they question their reasons for risking their lives. But in April 1945, British troops came across something that made it crystal clear why they were fighting. In a lonely forest, hidden from the world, the Germans had built a death camp full of unimaginable horrors.

When British soldiers entered the camp at Bergen-Belsen, in Germany, they found 60,000 men, women and children, trapped behind barbed-wire fences. Most of the prisoners were on the point of dying – from hunger, exhaustion or disease. Thousands had already collapsed and their bodies lay piled around the camp. The other prisoners were too weak to dig graves, and barely had the strength to eat, speak or stand as British medics struggled to help them.

Killing machine

Belsen was a concentration camp, one of hundreds the Nazis had set up across occupied Europe. Their chilling purpose was to imprison or murder anyone who didn't conform to the Nazi's insane vision of the world. Millions of Jews died in the camps, victims of the Nazi's racial prejudice. They were shot, gassed or worked to death by guards who had been taught that camp inmates were no better than wild animals.

On arrival at the camps, young children and old people were often gassed, because the guards considered them unfit for work. The rest of the prisoners were quickly stripped of their possessions and their identities, as other inmates shaved their heads and gave them ragged uniforms to wear. They lived on scraps of food, in constant fear for their lives. Few prisoners survived more than six months.

Ashes and dust

British medics worked day and night at Belsen, but thousands of the prisoners were too sick to be saved. Typhus fever was raging through the camp, so doctors evacuated the inmates to a local army base and burned the reeking prison to the ground. All that remained of Belsen was a smoking scar on the earth – a permanent reminder of the German Nazi party's mad and murderous hate.

At least six million Jews died in the concentration camps or were shot by Nazi killing squads. Their mass-murder is now known as the Holocaust.

Young victim

Anne Frank was a young Jewish German girl who kept an amazing diary of the years she spent hiding in Nazi-occupied Holland. She was betrayed and caught in 1944, and died at Belsen shortly before the British arrived.

Older than their years, these children are former inmates of Bergen-Belsen. They are waiting to receive soup from British troops. Some still wear their striped camp uniforms.

Defeating Germany

People walk past the once-triumphal Brandenburg Gate, which stands amid rubble and wreckage in the blasted German capital, Berlin.

While the Allies were advancing through France, Russian forces pressed in from the East – Germany had lost the war. But, like a trapped beast snarling and raging until the terrible end, Hitler ordered his soldiers to keep fighting. British troops had to battle harder than ever before they could finally celebrate a victory.

The bridge too far

While Hitler's armies kept on fighting, many German civilians struggled to survive. Left homeless and hungry by the war, this woman in Berlin is cooking for her family by the roadside.

In the summer of 1944, Allied commanders were hoping they could finish the war by Christmas. But the Allies stalled before the German's 'Siegfried Line' – a defensive belt of bunkers, minefields and barbed wire snaking along Germany's western border.

Montgomery came up with a plan to sidestep the Siegfried Line, by grabbing a series of vital bridges across the River Rhine, and then advancing into Germany. He sent paratroopers to capture bridges at Eindhoven, Nijmegen and Arnhem and keep them open for a column of his tanks. But the Germans stopped the column before it could reach the last bridge at Arnhem. After this disaster, the Allies advanced more cautiously, planning new attacks for spring 1945.

A last gasp

While the Allies settled in for a miserable Christmas, the battered remnants of the German army were gathering in the Ardennes forest. On December 16, they launched what became known as the Battle of the Bulge. It was a massive tank assault into Belgium, to try to break the Allied front and reach the sea. Almost 20,000 American soldiers died in the battle before the German attack was smashed.

To the bitter end

In March 1945, the Americans captured a bridge across the Rhine at Remagen. Montgomery's troops forced a crossing further north and the Allies raced into Germany. Realizing he was defeated, Hitler shot himself in his Berlin bunker, as Russian troops seized the city. On May 7, 1945, the head of the German armed forces ordered his men to surrender.

After over five years of struggle and suffering, the war in Europe was over. But Britain and the Allies still had to brace themselves for one last challenge – the battle with Japan.

Victory in Europe

Churchill declared May 8, Victory in Europe (VE) Day. He joined the Royal Family as they waved to the crowds from the balcony of Buckingham Palace.

In every town and village people hung out flags and drank toasts to their fighting men. Young and old, people celebrated with dances and street parties.

In this photograph, jubilant Londoners and British sailors celebrate VE Day with an impromptu street party.

Jungle fighters

A million British Commonwealth and empire troops fought in Burma. Some 120,000 of them came from Africa, and 700,000 were from India and Nepal.

Gurkha soldiers, from Nepal, are famed for their bravery and fighting skill. In battle, they carry a 46cm (18inch) knife, known as the *kukri*.

The sun sets on Japan

While millions of people celebrated peace in Europe, British troops were still fighting for their lives in Burma. The country's remote, impenetrable jungles were a terrifying battleground. Men struggled against disease, pounding heat, tropical storms and Japanese soldiers who would fight to the death rather than surrender.

Pulling back

After capturing Singapore, in 1942, Japanese forces had invaded nearby Burma and seized the capital, Rangoon. Burma's mountain ridges and rainforests protected the borders of India, Britain's most important colonial territory. But the Japanese advanced quickly, forcing the British to abandon most of their heavy equipment and retreat across almost a thousand miles of wild country.

British troops stopped the Japanese at the Indian frontier, but they had been badly mauled in the jungle, and were low on supplies. In contrast, Japanese soldiers had adapted well to the jungle, eating rodents, snakes and plants growing around them.

Rumble in the jungle

A maverick British commander, General Orde Wingate, formed a special jungle force to hit back at the enemy. Taking their name from a mythical beast, Wingate's *Chindits* marched deep into Burma and were supplied by mules and parachute airdrops.

After *Chindit* raids in 1943 and 1944, the British swept across Burma, overwhelming Japan's jungle troops. The Allies recaptured Rangoon in May, 1945, and made plans to invade Malaya. Allied armies were poised to attack Japan, but the country's leaders still refused to give in.

A final blow

On August 6, 1945, the Americans exploded a new and unimaginably destructive weapon over the Japanese city of Hiroshima – the atomic bomb. The city was reduced to dust, and over 80,000 civilians were killed. Only three days later, another bomb destroyed the city of Nagasaki. Japan's generals agreed to surrender on August 15. This date is remembered as VJ Day – victory in Japan.

At last, the Second World War was over.

Little Boy

The bomb that blasted Hiroshima was codenamed *Little Boy*.

The explosion caused a massive fireball that burned up everything within an area of 13 square km (5 square miles) and sent up a huge mushroom cloud of radioactive smoke.

A further 80,000 civilians died later of radiation poisoning, and many more people suffered sickness and disability as a result.

This photograph of Hiroshima was taken a few weeks after the city was almost completely flattened by an atomic bomb.

Out of the ashes

Counting the cost

At least sixty million soldiers and civilians died in the Second World War, more than in any other conflict.

Almost 400,000 British people lost their lives – including 60,000 civilians.

After more than five years of brutal war, the British people were exhausted. Thousands had died in air raids, in sinking ships and on lonely battlefields, and a million fathers and sons in uniform were still scattered around the world. It was time for the nation to heal its wounds and prepare for the future.

Some of Britain's soldiers had to wait months before their units stood down and they were shipped home. This process was known demobilization, or demob. But adjusting to civilian life after the war wasn't easy for everyone. Many returned to ruined homes and families they hadn't seen for a year or more.

A British soldier is cheered by local children, as he returns home.

60

The 1930s had been a time of unemployment and hardship for many people, but Britain's servicemen and women had risked their lives fighting for a better world. Now, they demanded jobs and more help from the government – and people across the country supported them.

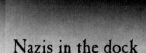

In it together

The British had learned a lot about themselves and their nation's problems since 1939. Men and women from all classes and backgrounds had trained, worked and struggled together to win the war. This national effort gave people a sense of unity and the confidence to make Britain a better place.

Wartime evacuations of children from city slums had opened people's eyes to the plight of the poor. Millions were living in squalor, with no chance of finding good schools or jobs and no health care if they became sick. People wanted to clear the slums and build a fairer society. They expected great things from their leaders.

A new team

In July, 1945, Churchill called an election. The man who had saved Britain from Hitler expected an easy victory for his Conservative Party. But Clement Attlee's Labour Party won the election by a landslide. Churchill was astonished. The voters would always respect their pugnacious war leader, but he moved into the shadows of history as the country prepared for the challenges of a new era.

Britain had helped win the war, but now the country had to face the new challenges of peacetime.

Nazis in the dock

Like Hitler himself, many Nazi leaders committed suicide before they could be caught by the Allies.

Those who survived were arrested and put on trial in the German city of Nuremberg. Most were found guilty of war crimes and sentenced to death.

This is one of the posters that helped the Labour Party to win the 1945 General Election.

Index

Acknowledgements

Every effort has been made to trace and acknowledge ownership of copyright. If any rights have been omitted, the publishers offer to rectify this in any future editions following notification. The publishers are grateful to the following individuals and organizations for their permission to reproduce material on the following pages: (t=top, b=bottom, m=middle, l=left, r=right)

cover (background) © Bettmann/Corbis, **(tl)** © Bettmann/Corbis, **(tr)** © David Wall/Alamy, **(ml)** © Hulton Archive/Getty Images, **(b)** IWM CH-000730 and ZZZ 8129C.

p1 IWM B 5103; **p2-3** © Bettmann/Corbis; **p6 (tl)** © Corbis (Heinrich Hoffmann); **p7** © Hulton Atchive/Getty Images; **p8 (bl)** IWM D651; **p9 (t)** The Art Archive/Eileen Tweedy, **(b)** © Eric Harlow/Hulton Archive/ 2007 Getty Images; **p11 (t)** Hulton Archive/2007 Getty Images; **p12** © Bettmann/Corbis; **p13 (t)** © David Low, Evening Standard, 14th May 1940, British Cartoon Archive, University of Kent; **p14** © Bert Hardy/Hulton Archive/2007 Getty Images; **p15 (tr)** © Popperfoto/Alamy; **p16 (b)** © Fox Photos/Hulton Archive/Getty Images; **p17 (t)** © Skyscan/Corbis; **p19** © David Pollack/Corbis; **p20-21** Keystone/Hulton Archive/2007 Getty Images; **p23** © Bettmann/Corbis; **p24 (bl)** © Corbis; **p24-25** © Bettmann/ Corbis; **p26 (tl)** © The Lordprice Collection/HIP/TopFoto; **p27** IWM D8806; **p28** © Zoltan Glass/Hulton Archive/Getty Images; **p29 (t)** © Keystone/Hulton Archive/Getty Images; **p30 (t)** © Keystone/Hulton Archive/Getty Images; **p31** © Keystone/Hulton Archive/Getty Images; **p32 (l)** IWM D23727; **p33 (br)** © Volker Steger/SPL; **p34** akg-images/ullstein bild; **p35 (t)** IWM A3532; **p36-37** © Corbis; **p37 (tr)** © Swim Ink 2, LLC/Corbis; **p38 (t)** akg-images/ullstein bild; **p39 (b)** Copy right © Ronald Searle 1943, by kind permission of the artist and The Sayle Literary Agency; **p40 (tl)** IWM E18980; **p40-41 (b)** © Popperfoto/Alamy; **p42** IWM FLM002343; **p43** IWM HU4594; **p44 (tl)** © The Art Archive/Eileen Tweedy; **p44-45** IWM C4363; **p46 (tl)** © ITV plc/Granada International/Source:BFI Stills, **(b)** IWM A14185; **p47 (t)** © Keystone/Hulton Archive Getty Images; **p48 (bl)** IWM MH3660; **p50-51** IWM B5245; **p52 (t)** © The Art Archive; **p53** IWM BU11149; **p55 (tr)** © Reuters/ Corbis, **(b)** © Keystone/Hulton Archive/Getty Images; **p56 (t)** © Keystone/Hulton Archive/ Getty Images, **(bl)** © Hulton-Deutsch Collection/Corbis; **p57 (b)** © Hulton Archive/Getty Images; **p58-59** © Corbis; **p59 (tr)** © John Van Hasselt/Corbis Sygma; **p60** © Hulton-Deutsch Collection/Corbis; **p61 (tr)** © Bettmann/Corbis, **(br)** © Museum of London.

Some of the photographs, both on the cover and inside this book, were originally in black and white and have been digitally tinted by Usborne Publishing. Some images have also been cropped for reasons of space.

For more information about the Imperial War Museum, go to **www.iwm.org.uk**

Digital design by John Russell; Picture research by Ruth King